Basics of ...

FLORIDA'S LANDLORD- TENANT LAW

Basics of ...

FLORIDA'S LANDLORD-TENANT LAW

An Explanation
For Everyday People

Albert L. Kelley, Esq.

Basics of ...
A Basic Knowledge Imprint of
ABSOLUTELY AMAZING eBOOKS

Basics of ...

is an imprint of
ABSOLUTELY AMAZING eBOOKS

Published by Whiz Bang LLC, 926 Truman Avenue, Key West, Florida 33040, USA

Basics of ... Florida Landlord-Tenant Law copyright © 2016 by Albert L. Kelley, Esq. Electronic compilation/ print edition copyright © 2016 by Whiz Bang LLC.

For information contact:
Publisher@AbsolutelyAmazingEbooks.com

ISBN-13: 978-1945772108 (Basics of ...)
ISBN-10: 1945772107

Basics of ...

FLORIDA'S LANDLORD-TENANT LAW

THANKS

This book was written with the help of my wonderful wife and first copy editor, Angie Kelley, who has been correcting my mistakes for over two decades.

Table of Contents

INTRODUCTION

Landlord-Tenant Law. Roughly one-third of Americans live in rental apartments. In addition, roughly one-sixth of the population are landlords. This means the total number of people affected by Landlord Tenant law is around 40% of the population. Eviction cases make up over 31% of all lawsuits filed in County Courts in Florida, second only to small claims actions.

With so many people affected by Landlord-Tenant Law, it is important to know what it is, how it works and what the procedures are. Luckily, most people will never have to go to Court, but that also means those who do will often be facing a stressful, confusing system and process that they are unfamiliar with. The purpose of this book is to remove some of the confusion and in turn to alleviate some of the stress.

Let me begin by giving you my background. My name is Al Kelley and I am a lawyer, magistrate, mediator, author, businessman, and book publisher. I spent several years as a college professor for St. Leo University. I graduated with honors from Florida State University in 1989 and have been practicing law ever since. During that time, I have handled cases focusing on business law, real estate, corporations, entertainment law, contracts, copyrights, and trademarks. I have represented landlords and tenants, and have worked for landlords who owned anywhere from one unit to entire apartment complexes. My clients have included individuals and companies. I have litigated countless Landlord-Tenant cases for both Landlords and Tenants. I have handled general civil litigation in the County, Circuit and Appellate Courts of Florida for both Plaintiff and Defendants. I have been a state certified mediator for over ten years and a Judicial Magistrate for two. I was also the Chairman of the Monroe County Career Service Council- a quasi-judicial agency. I am a member of the Florida Bar, and have been a member of the Trial Bar of the United States District Court for the Southern and Middle Districts of Florida. I also am the owner or co-owner of numerous companies. I have written a weekly newspaper column on the law for three different publications, as well as authoring two prior legal books, and teaching at numerous seminars. I have also been both a Landlord and a Tenant.

There are three types of Landlord-Tenant matters: Residential, Commercial and Self-Storage. This book will only deal with Residential. This is not an exhaustive treatise on how to litigate Landlord-Tenant cases. In law school students take an entire course on the Rules of Civil Procedure, another course on the rules of Evidence, another course on trial practice, and an entire year on research skills. I cannot condense the details of all of those courses into one manual. What this book does is lay out the basics of Residential Landlord-Tenant Laws. While I will discuss the Rules of Court, Evidence, Procedure and Research to some extent, this book cannot and does not replace legal advice and legal counsel.

Now for the mandatory disclaimer. The information being provided in this book is not designed to be specific legal advice. It is offered for information purposes only. It is not oriented towards any specific issue and through it, I am not representing any person or entity. The principles presented are based on Florida law (I am not licensed to practice in any other state and do not profess to be an expert on the laws of other states). If you have a specific legal issue that you need advice on, consult with an attorney of your choice.

I hope you find this book informative and entertaining, but mostly, I hope you find it useful.

THE LEASE

Every Landlord-Tenant matter starts with the Lease. Leases may be in writing or they may be verbal; basic or complex. But every rental requires some form of agreement. If the lease is verbal, the necessary terms for the lease, aside from the amount of rent and the dates rent is paid, will be determined by the statutes. With a written lease, many of the statutes can be bypassed, so that the written lease will be controlling. A verbal lease can be easier to terminate, but a written lease can provide more control and less obligation to the landlord.   So what terms do we need in a lease?

Property: This is usually pretty easy. Where is the property?   If it is in a multi-unit building, which unit is it? If leasing just a room, which room is it?   Does it include the yard?   What about storage sheds? Does it include common areas? If the lease requires explanation of the property, it should be in writing.

Parties: This is not always as it seems. Usually the property owner is the Landlord, but sometimes the Landlord is an agent of the property owner or even a tenant of the property owner.   The Tenant is also not always evident.   Although the landlord may negotiate with just one person, there can be others residing in the property.   If the main tenants have children, they are also considered tenants. In a verbal lease, pretty much anyone living in the property is a tenant. With a written lease, only those people identified in the lease are tenants; all others are guests of the tenant.

Term: This actually covers two issues: how long is the lease, and how often does the tenant have to pay rent. These clauses may be related. If the lease is going to be for a specific period of time, it needs to be in writing. If the lease is not in writing, it will be deemed terminable at will, and the length will be based on how often rent is paid. If the rent is paid on a weekly basis, the lease is said to be week-to-week; if on a monthly basis, it is month-to-month; and if on a yearly basis, it is year-to-year. These terms will become important if you have to proceed to eviction. If the lease is for more than a year, it must be in writing or it will be unenforceable under Florida's Statute of Frauds.

Rent: This is the most basic of issues. How much rent will the tenant have to pay? This is strictly a matter of negotiation. However, this clause also determines how the rent is paid. Can it be paid in cash, check or cashier's check? Where is the payment delivered? Can the tenant make a direct deposit into the Landlord's bank account?

Security Deposit: Of all the terms in a lease, this one probably gets more Landlords in trouble and causes more fights than any other item. So let's spend a few minutes on it. First, if a Landlord is going to require a security deposit, it is recommended that they have a written lease. The statues have specific requirements regarding security deposits and while many statues may be bypassed with a written lease, the security deposit laws may not. Even with a written lease, the security deposit statutes must be complied with. But, a written lease will assist the Landlord in complying with the statutes. Unless specified otherwise in a written lease, the security deposit is only to repair damage to the property after the tenant vacates. Many landlords believe they can apply security deposit to past due rents. That is a sure fire way to go to court. And lose. If the Landlord has five or more rental units, specific language MUST be included in the lease. The Statute requires that the following be included in the lease: YOUR LEASE REQUIRES PAYMENT OF CERTAIN DEPOSITS. THE LANDLORD MAY TRANSFER ADVANCE RENTS TO THE LANDLORD'S ACCOUNT AS THEY ARE DUE AND WITHOUT NOTICE. WHEN YOU MOVE OUT, YOU MUST GIVE THE LANDLORD YOUR NEW ADDRESS SO THAT THE LANDLORD CAN SEND YOU NOTICES REGARDING YOUR DEPOSIT. THE LANDLORD MUST MAIL YOU NOTICE, WITHIN 30 DAYS AFTER YOU MOVE OUT, OF THE LANDLORD'S INTENT TO IMPOSE A CLAIM AGAINST THE DEPOSIT. IF YOU DO NOT REPLY TO THE LANDLORD STATING YOUR OBJECTION TO THE CLAIM WITHIN 15 DAYS AFTER RECEIPT OF THE LANDLORD'S NOTICE, THE LANDLORD WILL COLLECT THE CLAIM AND MUST MAIL YOU THE REMAINING DEPOSIT, IF ANY.

IF THE LANDLORD FAILS TO TIMELY MAIL YOU NOTICE, THE LANDLORD MUST RETURN THE DEPOSIT BUT MAY LATER FILE A LAWSUIT AGAINST YOU FOR DAMAGES. IF YOU FAIL TO TIMELY OBJECT TO A CLAIM, THE LANDLORD MAY COLLECT FROM THE DEPOSIT, BUT YOU MAY LATER FILE A LAWSUIT CLAIMING A REFUND.

YOU SHOULD ATTEMPT TO INFORMALLY RESOLVE ANY DISPUTE BEFORE FILING A LAWSUIT. GENERALLY, THE PARTY IN WHOSE FAVOR A JUDGMENT IS RENDERED WILL BE AWARDED COSTS AND ATTORNEY FEES PAYABLE BY THE LOSING PARTY.

THIS DISCLOSURE IS BASIC. PLEASE REFER TO PART II OF CHAPTER 83, FLORIDA STATUTES, TO DETERMINE YOUR

LEGAL RIGHTS AND OBLIGATIONS.

The statutes further states: "Upon the vacating of the premises for termination of the lease, if the landlord does not intend to impose a claim on the security deposit, the landlord shall have 15 days to return the security deposit together with interest if otherwise required, or the landlord shall have 30 days to give the tenant written notice by certified mail to the tenant's last known mailing address of his or her intention to impose a claim on the deposit and the reason for imposing the claim. The notice shall contain a statement in substantially the following form:

This is a notice of my intention to impose a claim for damages in the amount of   upon your security deposit, due to

_____. It is sent to you as required by s.
83.49(3), Florida Statutes. You are hereby notified that you must object in writing to this deduction from your security deposit within 15 days from the time you receive this notice or I will be authorized to deduct my claim from your security deposit. Your objection must be sent to _____ (landlord's address)."

Security deposits are to be held in a separate bank account which can be interest bearing or non-interest bearing. If interest bearing, the Landlord must pay interest to the Tenant. The Landlord cannot comingle security deposit monies with any other monies.

Maintenance: The statutes set out maintenance requirements for both the Landlord and the Tenant. Under the statutes, most of the maintenance obligations fall to the Landlord. If you only have a verbal lease, these statutes control.   The landlord must maintain the roofs, windows, doors, floors, steps, porches, exterior walls, foundations, and all other structural components in good repair, keep the plumbing in reasonable working condition, ensure that screens are installed in a reasonable condition and repair damage to them once a year. In addition, the Landlord must make reasonable provisions for extermination services, provision of locks and keys, cleaning the common areas, garbage removal and functioning facilities for heat during winter, running water, and hot water. He must also install working smoke detection devices. If the Landlord gives the Tenant a written lease, all of the above can be changed. If the lease addresses maintenance issues, the lease will overrule the statute. In fact, the lease can actually place all maintenance obligations on the Tenant.

LEASE TERMINATION

How to terminate a lease is one of the most frequent questions landlords ask. The way to terminate a lease depends primarily on why it is being terminated. It also depends on the type of lease and the terms of the lease.

A written lease for a specific term (such as six months) will terminate when the term of the lease ends. In other words, at the end of six months, the Tenant must vacate the premises unless the Landlord allows them to stay after the lease or unless they obtain a new lease. If the tenant fails to vacate the premises at the end of the lease, the Landlord is entitled to file an immediate eviction action (The eviction process will be discussed in the next Chapter).

If the lease does not have a specific term, or if it is a verbal lease, it is deemed a lease at will and can be terminated at any time, subject to the statutory notice provisions. The notice provisions are based upon the payment of rent. If rent is paid on a weekly basis, it is a week-to-week lease. Either party, Landlord or Tenant, may terminate the lease by giving the other party written notice of termination at least one week before termination. If rent is paid on a monthly basis (the most common), it is called a month-to-month lease and may be terminated by either party by giving written notice at least 15 days before the end of the rental period. If rent is paid on a quarterly basis (every three months) the lease is quarter-to-quarter and may be terminated by either party by giving written notice at least 30 days before the end of the rental period. If rent is paid on an annual basis, it is referred to as year-to-year and either party may terminate it by giving written notice at least 60 days before the end of the rental period.

There is no special language that needs to be in the written notice; just a written statement that the party intends to terminate the lease at the end of the rental period.

I want to be clear about the notification period. As mentioned before, the vast majority of residential leases are month-to-month and most Landlords are familiar with the phrase 15-day notice. But often they do not understand the meaning of that phrase. Many Landlords believe they can terminate a month-to-month lease at any time so long as they give the tenant 15 days' notice. In other words, the Landlord believes they can give the 15-day notice at any time and 15 days later the Tenant must leave. This is incorrect. If rent is paid on the 1st of the month, the Landlord MUST give the notice at least 15 days before the 1st. But no matter how early it is given, the lease cannot be terminated before the 1st. If the Landlord gives the notice less than 15 days before the end of the rental period, it is not effective until the end of the next rental period. In other words, a notice given after the 16th for a 30-day month or the 17th for a 31-day month will not be effective until the end of the following month. Many eviction cases have been lost because the Landlord did not give the proper notice.

Leases can be terminated during their term if there is a breach of the lease agreement. The most common breach is the nonpayment of rent.   If a tenant fails to pay rent, the day after the rent is due the Landlord can deliver to the tenant what is termed a Three-Day Notice To Pay Rent or Vacate.   The three-day notice is a specific form dictated by the statutes. The wording is: *You are hereby notified that you are indebted to me in the sum of   dollars for the rent and use of the premises (address of leased premises, including county), Florida, now occupied by you and that I demand payment of the rent or possession of the premises within 3 days (excluding Saturday, Sunday, and legal holidays) from the date of delivery of this notice, to wit: on or before the   day of ,   (year) .* (A copy is attached at the end of this book in the Appendix).   The notice must be signed by the Landlord and his name and address must be at the bottom. The Notice must be served on the Tenant either by personal delivery, or if the Tenant is not home, by posting the notice on the front door of the rental unit.   After the Three Day Notice has been served on the Tenant, the Tenant can cure the breach by paying the rent to the Landlord. During the three-day period (again, excluding the day of service, weekends and legal holidays), if the Tenant attempts to pay the rent to the Landlord, the Landlord MUST accept it.   Refusal to accept the rent gives the Tenant a defense to an eviction action.   However, the Landlord does not have to accept anything less than full rent.   In other words, if the Tenant offers to pay a portion of the rent within the three days and the remainder afterwards, the Landlord may lawfully refuse to accept it. At the end of the three days, if the Tenant attempts to pay the rent, the Landlord may lawfully refuse to accept the rent and proceed with eviction.

There are other ways to breach a lease, and the type of breach will determine how the lease gets terminated. Most of the time, these are issues that arise under written leases, as verbal leases are governed by statute and therefore only statutory violations would be deemed breaches. If the breach of the lease is minor where the Tenant should be given the right to correct the violation, such as when there are unauthorized guests in the apartment, or the Tenant has pets without permission, or has unregistered cars in the parking area, then the Landlord must give the Tenant a seven-day Notice to Cure in substantially the following format: *You are hereby notified that (cite the noncompliance). Demand is hereby made that you remedy the noncompliance within 7 days of receipt of this notice or your lease shall be deemed terminated and you shall vacate the premises upon such termination. If this same conduct or conduct of a similar nature is repeated within 12 months, your tenancy is subject to termination without further warning and without your being given an opportunity to cure the noncompliance.* (A copy of the 7 Day Notice to Cure is attached at the end of this book in the Appendix). If the violation is not cured or once cured recurs within the next twelve months, then the Landlord is allowed to proceed with eviction. If the Tenant does cure the violation, then the lease continues as if there had been no breach (unless the violation recurs during the next twelve months).

Where the violation is more severe and is of such a character that the Tenant should not be given the right to cure (Examples include damage to the property, threats to other tenants, and repeat violations), the Landlord must give the Tenant a seven-day Notice to Vacate in substantially the following format: *You are advised that your lease is terminated effective immediately. You shall have 7 days from the delivery of this letter to vacate the premises. This action is taken because (cite the noncompliance).* (A more detailed version of the 7 Day Notice to Vacate is attached at the end of the book in the Appendix). Because this Notice is only issued for severe violations, the Tenant cannot simply cure the breach but is required to vacate the premises, even if the rent is current.

Leases can also be breached by the Landlord. Usually this occurs when the Landlord fails to maintain the property appropriately. For example, if the roof develops a leak, the Landlord has an obligation to repair the leak. If he doesn't, that is a breach. The Tenant must be proactive if the Landlord breaches the Lease, but they must also follow the statutory procedures. If the Tenant waits until the Landlord files an eviction action against the Tenant, it is too late for the Tenant to use the noncompliance as a defense. A breach by the Landlord for failure to maintain the premises may not be used as a defense to an eviction case. Therefore, the Tenant wants to act before the Landlord starts an eviction action.

If the Landlord fails to maintain the premises, the Tenant has an obligation to give the Landlord a seven-day written notice of the non-compliance. The seven-day notice must specify the non-compliance and advise that the Tenant intends to terminate the lease if it is not corrected. There is no special language for the notice.

If the cause of the non-compliance is due to causes outside the control of the Landlord and the Landlord makes timely and reasonable efforts to correct the noncompliance, the parties may either terminate the Lease or modify the Lease. The modification depends on the severity of the problem. If the damage is such that the property is uninhabitable, then the Tenant is not responsible for payment of the rent until the damage is repaired, however, the Tenant cannot live in the property (It cannot be uninhabitable and be lived in at the same time). If the damage does not make the property uninhabitable, but reduces the value of the property, the rent shall be reduced accordingly.

For each of the above breaches by Landlord or Tenant, the Notices must be delivered directly to the breaching party by mail or actual delivery of a true copy. However, if the Tenant is not at home when the Landlord attempts to serve him, the Landlord may simply post a copy of the Notice on the front door. You cannot waive any of the Notice provisions in the Lease.

THE LAW

To understand Landlord-Tenant issues, it is advisable to first understand some basic legal principles. First is to know where to find the laws that govern Landlord-Tenant cases. There are numerous sources of law. The premier source is the Constitution. Not only do we have a Constitution for the United States, each state also has a Constitution. These documents are the cornerstone of all our laws. Their purpose is to set out the basic legal theories for their citizens and legislatures to follow. Therefore, they cannot be changed by statutes or the legislature; only by a vote of the people. Generally, Landlord-Tenant cases are not based on Constitutional law.

Next we have the statutes, both state and federal. These are the laws passed by the state and federal legislatures. These laws regulate the activities of the citizens of the states and their local governments. There are currently approximately 48 Titles in the Florida Statutes, covering nearly 1,000 chapters, and likely tens of thousands of laws.

Related to statutes are ordinances. These are the laws passed by lower government agencies such as the City and County Commissions. They only apply to the citizens who live in their districts. Generally, these are not applicable to Landlord-Tenant cases, unless the violation of an ordinance has caused a breach of the lease.

The next section of laws is the administrative

regulations, such as the Internal Revenue Code. Administrative regulations are governed by the various administrative agencies such as the Securities and Exchange Commission, the National Labor Relations Board, and the Department of Business and Professional Regulation. These regulations have the weight of statutes, but are enforced by the agencies rather than the Courts. Again, it is highly unlikely that an administrative law might be the basis of a Landlord-Tenant case.

As for the Courts, they are our next source of law. Decisions of the appellate courts, what we refer to as "Caselaw", has the weight of statutes. When the Court publishes its decision on a case, that decision becomes the law for all similarly situated cases before that court and all lower courts (Decisions do not control higher courts. In other words, the Supreme Court is not controlled by the decisions of the Appellate Courts, and the Appellate Courts are not controlled by the Circuit Courts. One of the purposes of the higher courts is to review the decisions of the lower courts). This is the theory of "stare decisis" (literally, to stand by the decision). Prior decisions set precedent for all future courts to follow until the decision is reversed by a higher court. The difficulty here is that there are hundreds of years of caselaw to research and it is often difficult to find the cases that support your argument. However, almost every case you will bring in court will be similar to a case that has been heard before, and caselaw is a great resource to use to build your case.

Next we have the common law. These are rules and principles that derive their authority solely from custom and usage. Florida law is based on the laws of England.

When the Florida Legislative Council first met in 1845, one of the first things they did was to adopt the "common law" as it existed in England on July 4, 1776. These laws were not written in statute books but came from Court decisions, some of which are more than 800 years old. On top of that, the State also looked to Spanish laws from the years under Spanish rule (There are Spanish laws that reach back to 1597). Today, the common law is still not found in the statute books, but is followed and can be enforced, although, this is only rarely invoked in Landlord-Tenant cases.

So how do all of these sources of law affect you? Because the courts act under the theory of stare decisis, if you can find a prior case that has the same issues as your case, or if you can find a statute that addresses your situation, it will heavily influence the Judge's decision. Ideally, this research would be done before you file your case or your answer so you know where you stand before you waste time and money. The question is, how do you find it?

In today's electronic world, legal research is easier than ever, although that does not mean easy. The Florida Constitution and Statutes are readily available online. The Florida Legislature has posted them online at www.leg.state.fl.us and you can find them through other sites as well. While there is a search feature on the legislature's website, unless you know specifically how to phrase your search terms, it may give you an excessive amount of laws to review. It may be easier to start with a review of the Titles in the Table of Contents and then when you find one that looks like it may affect your case, read the chapters inside. Unfortunately, the terms used in the Table of Contents can be confusing. As an example, while it would seem appropriate to find Florida's Landlord-Tenant laws in Title 40 under Real and Personal Property, that would be wrong. Florida's Landlord-Tenant law falls under Title 6-Civil Practice and Procedure, specifically Chapter 83, Section 2.

As an aside, Title VII-Limitations at Chapter 95-Limitations of Actions; Adverse Possession should be reviewed in EVERY case. This is the statute of limitations and will let you know how long you have to bring a suit. For example, a lawsuit based on a written contract must be brought within 5 years, but for a verbal contract, within 4 years. After those time periods, the lawsuit is improper and can be thrown out. While the Statue of Limitations does not generally affect eviction cases, it does affect when a Landlord may file for back rent or when a tenant can file for return of deposits or either party filing a claim for the improper taking of personal items.

Aside from the above, other cases that have a five-year statute of limitations include foreclosure cases and non-payment of minimum wage. Four-year statute of limitations applies also to (among other things):

- negligence actions
- an action based on the design
- planning, or construction of an improvement to real property
- an action to recover public money or property held by a public officer or employee
- an action for injury based on the design,

manufacture, distribution, or sale of personal property
- an action founded on a statutory liability
- an action for taking, detaining, or injuring personal property
- an action to recover specific personal property
- a legal or equitable action founded on fraud
- an action to rescind a contract
- an action for money paid to any governmental authority by mistake or inadvertence
- an action for a statutory penalty or forfeiture or an action for assault, battery, false arrest, malicious prosecution, malicious interference, false imprisonment, or any other intentional tort.

Florida also has a two-year statute of limitation for, among other things:
- an action for professional malpractice
- an action to recover wages or overtime
- an action for wrongful death
- and an action for libel or slander

Lastly, there is a one-year statute of limitations for:
- an action for specific performance of a contract
- an action to enforce an equitable lien arising from the furnishing of labor, services, or material for the improvement of real property
- an action to enforce rights under a Letter of Credit
- an action against any guaranty association
- an action to enforce any claim against a payment bond on which the principal is a contractor,

subcontractor, or sub-subcontractor

- an action to enforce a claim of a deficiency related to a note secured by a mortgage against a residential property that is a one-family to four-family dwelling unit.

Many times it is difficult just to know what Title in the Florida Statutes to look at. Here your search engines (Google, Bing, etc.) are helpful. A simple search for "Florida Landlord/Tenant law" can provide a number of starting points for your research, including what statutes to review. The other difficulty is that there may be statutes which put specific requirements that can limit your recovery. As an example, Florida has a statute called the Statute of Frauds (Florida Statutes 725). This has nothing to do with fraud as most of us know it. The statute states that in certain circumstances a contract must be written to be valid. Generally, in Florida the contracts covered under the Statute of Frauds include any contract made in consideration of marriage; any lease for longer than a year; any guarantee or assurance made by a health care provider as to the results of any medical, surgical, or diagnostic procedure performed by any physician, osteopathic physician, chiropractic physician, podiatric physician, or dentist; for any contract that cannot be completed within one year; any contract for sale of land; and any contract where one person agrees to pay the debts of another person, living or dead. If any of these contracts are made by verbal agreement, they are not enforceable. The writing required by the Statute of Frauds doesn't require a formal written agreement, signed and notarized. It may be merely a memorandum stating the terms. So long as it is signed by the party it is being used against and contains all of the terms of the agreement, it may be sufficient.

A Statute of Frauds contract is generally voidable, not void. It is what we call an affirmative defense. In other words, it must be specifically pled as a defense at the beginning of a lawsuit or it cannot later be raised. As an affirmative defense, it does not deny the debt or obligation; it just says the debt cannot be enforced.

As you can see, it is important to fully research your claim (or your defense). You should expect to spend several hours, just on the research.

Unfortunately, caselaw is much harder to research than the statutes if you are not a lawyer. Years ago, each County had a county law library, usually located at the County Courthouse where the case books were readily available. This was a major expense as the books are updated on a regular basis and new casebooks are issued every year. These days, the books are usually no longer maintained by the County and research is done almost exclusively online. For lawyers, there are caselaw search services such as Fastcase and Westlaw that allow us to find cases rapidly. These are usually pay services that charge a subscription fee for their use. For the layperson, it is not as easy. Check with your local County Library to see if they provide a free online legal research center. If not, the search engines can also be helpful. Major cases can be found online, but lesser cases can be difficult (The County Library may have the statute and case books, but make sure they are updated. Nothing is worse than going to Court and using a case that was overturned the week before).

You want to search for cases that are similar to yours

and have the same basic facts. Most cases are written in the same format: Facts, Issues, Rationale, and Holding. The facts are just that: the facts of that particular case. By reviewing the beginning of most cases you can tell rapidly if the case is at all similar to yours. Issues are the question that this particular Court is trying to answer. Even if the facts are similar to yours, the Court may only be answering a specific question that has no bearing on your case. Rationale is the theories that the Court uses to reach their answer and Holding is the final decision of the Court. Be careful in reading the Holding. In some cases, there will be a majority opinion which is the actual holding, but another appellate judge may disagree and issue a dissenting opinion. This is not the law, but an explanation why he thinks the other judges got it wrong. Nothing is more embarrassing and will lose your case faster than citing a dissenting opinion as if it were the law (except citing an overturned decision).

While I can't teach legal research in this book (law schools spend an entire year teaching students how to do legal research, and the skills needed are developed only through years of practice), I will attempt to give a thumbnail sketch.

First, the books. When dealing with Florida law, if you don't have access to the internet, there are five sets of books to be intimately familiar with. First are the Florida Statutes (Annotated if possible- the FSA). The Annotated Statutes is a series of books that detail the Florida statutes in numerical order (There are over 900 chapters in the Florida Statutes and each Chapter has numerous statutes). After publishing the statute, the book then lists a basic history of the current version of the statute and provides a thumbnail sketch of some cases that have interpreted it. The FSA is very easy to use and comes with a very comprehensive set of index books. The statutes and annotations are updated annually in what is referred to as a "pocket part" which is a booklet that is inserted into the back cover of the book. After reviewing the statute, you should be sure to look in the pocket part to see if the law has been modified or deleted. While the annotation may be helpful in clarifying the law, you should never trust the annotation to be correct. When doing research, you should always read the complete case to ensure that it says what the annotation indicates. Occasionally, the annotation will be wrong.

The second set of books are called "Southern Reporter". There are actually three series of Southern Reporters. The first encompasses two hundred volumes covering cases before 1941; the second series covers cases from 1941-2008 and the third series covers cases after 2008. These books hold all of the reported cases from the Florida Supreme Court and the Florida Courts of Appeal. This is where most of Florida law comes from. The books are not easy to use unless you know what case you are looking for. While the books have small topic references in them, there are other books, which I will discuss shortly, that are better for looking up topics. The Southern Reporters are best used once you know which case you want to read. Cases are cited by the book and page number where they are located along with the Court and year they were decided. For example, a citation that reads: <u>Key West Polo Club Developers, Inc. v Tower Const. Co. of Panama City, Inc.</u>, 589 So.2d 917 (Fla. 3DCA 1991) tells us that the case involved the two parties

Key West Polo Club Developers, Inc. and Tower Construction Company of Panama City, Inc., that it was decided by the Third District Court of Appeals in 1991, and that a copy of the case can be found in volume 589 of the Southern Reporter, 2nd Series, at page 917. These cases tell you what the Courts have said about the law. The Courts rulings are binding on all lower Courts in the same district (the Circuit Courts must follow the rulings of the District Court of Appeals, which must follow the rulings of the Supreme Court). However, just because a case says what you want it to say, it may not be the law.

The third set of books is the Shepard's Citations. Shepard's is little more than a book full of numbers and abbreviations, but those abbreviations tell what the current status of a case is. For this reason, Shepard's is one of the most important research tools available. Shepard's Citations lists every case that has been reported in Southern Reporters (all three series) and then lists every subsequent case that has mentioned it, indicating which portion of the first case was discussed, whether it was in the main opinion or a dissenting opinion, whether the original case was followed or overruled, and which Courts have addressed the case. Without showing you the books, it is difficult to describe, but I will make an effort.

Referring to the case <u>Smetal Corp. v West Lake Inv. Co.</u>, 172 So. 58 (Fla. S.Ct. 1936). This is a very old case and has been mentioned at some point by every appellate court in Florida. Under Shepard's Citations, I looked this case up, first based on its book and page number. Occasionally, there will be two cases published on the same page, and Shepard's will indicate this as well. In my example case, it was the only case on that page. Shepard's then lists by book and page number all of the cases that cited <u>Smetal Corp</u>, starting with those cases from the Supreme Court, then the Florida Appellate Courts in numerical order (1ˢᵗ, 2ⁿᵈ, 3ʳᵈ, 4ᵗʰ, and 5ᵗʰ), and then the Federal Circuit Courts in numerical order. Next to some of the cases will be a letter. These letters tell how the following court referenced the cited case. The letters are as follows: a (affirmed), cc (connected case), D (dismissed), m (modified), r (reversed), s (same case), S (superseded), v (vacated), c (criticized), d (distinguished), e (explained), f (followed), h (harmonized), j (dissenting opinion), L (limited), o (overruled), p (parallel), and q (questioned). These letters are crucial as a case that has been reversed or overruled may no longer be good law. Also a case cited in a dissenting opinion may conflict with the controlling decision. In the <u>Smetal Corp.</u> case, 8 court decisions had distinguished the case, two had followed it, and one had mentioned it in a dissenting opinion. Also next to the listed cases may be a comment such as "note 1". This refers to the "Headnote". At the beginning of the cases as published in the Reporters, you will see a group of small numbered paragraphs, summarizing the major points of the case. These are the headnotes. Often, you will only be interested in one particular point of the case. Shepard's lets you see which cases referred specifically to that headnote, so you don't have to look up other cases that are irrelevant to your issue. The <u>Smetal Corp.</u> case had over 24 headnotes. Every case that is looked up should be Shepardized, if for no other reason than to ensure that it has not been overruled.

The reason for headnotes isn't simply to give you a

summary of that case, but to allow you to find other cases that address the same issue. Each headnote is preceded by a topic and what is referred to as a "key number". Key numbers are assigned to each topic and subtopic, to group cases together that cover the same points. Key numbers are issued by the West Publishing Company.

Not only does West Publishing Company publish the Southern Reporter series of cases, but also a series of books called West's Digest. The Digest is a collection of the headnotes listed according to key number. In other words, if you find a case that refers to the necessity of obtaining personal service on a party to a lawsuit, it will give a keynote of "48" under the topic of "Process". This keynote refers to the subtopic of "Nature and Necessity in General". To find more cases that address this same issue, you would refer to West's Digest, look up the section on "Process" and then turn to section 48. Here would be a listing of headnotes from other cases that refer to the same point. Each headnote states the citation of the case it comes from, allowing the reader to locate other cases that may benefit their position.

To keep the Digests updated, there is a small pouch in the back cover of each issue. Here is inserted a booklet called a "pocket-part" (discussed earlier) which contains new headnotes issued since the last edition of the book was released. It is helpful to review the pocket-part after reviewing the digest itself to get the more up-to-date cases and to see if there are cases that seem to reverse prior holdings.

Of course, as I mentioned before, you cannot rely on the headnotes alone. Occasionally, a headnote itself will be incorrect. It is crucial that the actual case be fully read to ensure that the headnote is correct. After the case is reviewed, you must again "Shepardize" it (as described earlier) to ensure that the case has not been overturned, questioned, or reversed.

The last major book series to be familiar with is Florida Jurisprudence Second Series (referred to as Fla. Jur. 2d). This is a great book for summarizing general legal points. Fla. Jur. 2d is divided into various legal issues, and then each issue is subdivided into various points and sub-issues. Rather than simply list cases or headnotes, Fla. Jur. 2d is written in narrative style so that it is reader friendly. Those interested in learning the state of the law can simply read sections of Fla. Jur. 2d as if they were reading any textbook. As a research tool, Fla. Jur. 2d is a great asset. Throughout each narrative paragraph, Fla. Jur. 2d has numerous footnotes, citing to the cases that they relied upon for their information. However, as with the headnotes, it is important not to simply take Fla. Jur. 2d at face value, but to actually read the cases. They may not actually state exactly what Fla. Jur. 2d says they do. And like with the Digests, Fla. Jur. 2d is updated routinely with pocket parts.

It should be noted that neither the Digests nor Fla. Jur. 2d are actual statements of the law, but should be used as reference material to find the law.

A final series that I want to mention are the Florida Law Weekly series. This is not actually a book set, but a series of booklets which contain those cases that were published by West Publishing Company during the previous week by the Supreme Court and all District Courts of Appeal. Because they are printed on a weekly basis, it is difficult to research through Fla. Law Weekly, but it is important that these cases be reviewed because at any time, a new case may overturn an older one. The last thing anyone wants to do is to give the judge a case that has been overturned.

If you live near a major city in Florida, you can locate these books at one of the University Law Schools (there are currently 12 ABA accredited law schools in Florida: Ave Maria School of Law (Naples); Barry University School of Law (Orlando); Florida A&M University College of Law (Orlando); Florida Coastal School of Law (Jacksonville); Florida International University College of Law (Miami); Florida State University College of Law (Tallahassee); Nova Southeastern University (Ft Lauderdale); Stetson University College of Law (Gulfport); St. Thomas University School of Law (Miami Gardens); Thomas M. Cooley Law School, Tampa Bay Campus (Riverview); University of Florida Levin College of Law (Gainesville); and University of Miami School of Law (Coral Gables). If a law school is not available, check with your local community college to see if they carry these books.

Online resources exist if the books are not available, but for non-lawyers, the search capability is not optimum. Some of the websites available are Findlaw.com, law.justia.com, Google Scholar (scholar.google.com), and the Public Library of Law (plol.org). In addition, most appellate courts throughout the country publish their own opinions online. These legal search engines will assist with doing legal research, however, it may take time to develop the skills to do it quickly. Most online sites will let you search by the name of one of the parties, lawyers or judges, or by searching dates or keywords. Online research on these sites is often not as fast as research with books due to the search engine limitations. The difficulty is defining the issue you want to research. If your search is too broad, you will get back hundreds or thousands of responses; if too narrow, you may not get the response you need. For example, on Google Scholar, I searched "Landlord Tenant". I received back 89,000 responses. When I put the search into quotation marks ("landlord tenant"), I received 25,300 responses. When I added "breach", I received just 7,850 responses. As you can see, you will want to narrow your search as much as possible. Even with the best keyword search, be prepared to spend a great deal of time reading many cases that will have nothing to do with your situation.

If you can research the statutes and caselaw, you will have a much stronger case to present.

STARTING AN EVICTION ACTION

Before filing an eviction action, the Landlord needs to determine if they want to just get rid of the Tenant or if they also want to sue for the unpaid back rent. This changes how the case is filed and how much it cost. We will start with just the eviction and address back rent later.

To file an eviction action, a Complaint needs to be filed with the Clerk of Court. The Complaint needs to allege the address of the property, state that the Landlord owns the property, advise if the lease is written or verbal, advise why the Tenant is being evicted and advise that the appropriate Notice was served. If the lease is written, a copy must be attached to the Complaint. The Landlord must also attach a copy of the Notice (3, 7 or 15 day). These attachments are crucial. If the Lease and Notice are not attached, the Complaint "fails to state a cause of action". This is a legal phrase that essentially means that the landlord has not alleged all of the things necessary for the Court to rule on his case. If the Complaint fails to state a cause of action, the Court should dismiss it. The Landlord can use the terms Plaintiff and Defendant rather than Landlord and Tenant, but most Courts will allow the less formal titles to be used. Also, the Landlord should be the party filing the Complaint. This seems obvious, but often real estate agents will file an eviction action for their clients. While the statute allows the agent to file the Complaint, they cannot do anything more in the case unless they are also an attorney. The real estate agent is not the Landlord and has no standing to pursue the case on the Landlord's behalf ("Standing" is a legal term meaning the right of a person to be before the Court. It is a question of whether the person is legally entitled to have the Court determine their case. The real estate agent is not the Landlord, but merely a third-party beneficiary of the Landlord's lease. This is not sufficient to let them file the action).

If the Landlord merely wants to evict the Tenant, all that is required is to file is a Complaint and a five-day Summons and pay the appropriate filing fee (In Monroe County, the filing fee is $185, plus $0 for each summons). If you also want to seek back rent, you have to add a separate count to the eviction Complaint, a five-day Summons and a 20-day Summons and pay a higher filing fee (The filing fee in Monroe County for an eviction with back rent is $300 plus $10 for each summons). In the Appendix to this book, I have included drafts forms for the Complaint, the 5 Day Summons and the 20 Day Summons.

Eviction matters are always County Court cases. They are covered by the Rules of Civil Procedure and are generally heard by a County Court Judge (In Florida, there are four types of trial Judges- County Court Judges, Circuit Court Judges, Appellate Court Judges and Supreme Court Justices. There are also magistrates and administrative judges. Administrative judges handle matters for various governmental agencies and do not get involved in Landlord Tenant cases. Occasionally the County Court will employ magistrates to hear certain cases to assist the Judges. The magistrates [also sometimes referred to as Special Masters] do not rule on the case, but merely make a recommendation to the Judge who will issue a ruling based on the recommendation). Rarely will the Courts use magistrates for Eviction actions. The Legislature intended for evictions to occur quickly and passed statutes requiring eviction cases to be expedited. As the parties before a magistrate have 10 days to file oppositions to the Magistrate's ruling, this would delay the eviction action for another week and a half.

After the Clerk issues the Summons, it must be delivered to the local Sheriff's Office. In some Counties the Sheriff will also require the Landlord to provide a map showing where the property is located (In Monroe County, they ask for a copy of the Property Appraiser's website showing the property to be served). Landlord's should also provide a self-addressed stamped envelope so the Sheriff's Office can send proof of service which may be necessary if the Tenant does not respond.

The Sheriff's Deputy will make three attempts to serve the Tenant. If on the third attempt the Tenant still does not answer the door, the Sheriff's Deputy will post the Summons on the door. If it gets torn off or blown away, it doesn't matter- the Tenant has still been served.

Once the Tenant has been served with the lawsuit, they have five business days to respond. Just as with the Notices, the day of service, Saturday, Sunday and legal holidays are not counted. To respond, the Tenant needs to address the Complaint directly and either admit or deny the Landlord's allegations. The response to the Complaint is called the "Answer". There is no specific form that the Answer must follow; any response will be accepted by the Court, so long as it is responsive to the allegations in the Complaint. If the Tenant has any defenses, this is also the time to bring them up. Defenses are listed under the title "Affirmative Defenses". The rules require defenses to be listed in the initial pleading; if the tenant fails to bring them up, they are deemed waived. That being said, these proceedings are less formal than most court cases, so some Courts will allow defenses to be raised for the first time at trial.

If the reason the Tenant is being evicted is non-payment of rent the Tenant must also pay the rent alleged to be owed to the Clerk of the Court. There are only two exceptions: if the Tenant's defense is that he already paid the rent, the rent does not need to be paid to the Clerk. Also, if the Tenant believes he should not have to pay the full rent, or dispute the amount the Landlord has alleged, the Tenant can ask the Court to determine how much rent should be paid. The Court will review the grounds the Tenant alleges and make a determination as to the amount of rent that is due. The tenant must pay this amount, plus file their answer to the Complaint before the hearing on the eviction Complaint.

The Court expedites these cases. So the Court will schedule the eviction hearing as soon as possible. This should not be taken lightly. This is a trial. The parties should be prepared.

MOTION PRACTICE

When most people think of lawsuits, they think of trials. However, the best lawyers don't always win cases at trial; often cases are won during what is referred to as Motion Practice. A lot of things are handled by Motion. In fact, there are so many possible motions that can be filed, it would take too much room to discuss it in too much detail. Here I will just discuss some of the main motions filed in an eviction case.

A Motion is a request that the Court make a decision about a contested issue. It may be instructional or limiting. It may be positive or negative. The person who files a Motion in referred to as "the Moving Party"; the opposing side is referred to as "the Nonmoving Party". Because an eviction case moves quickly, there are few reasons to file a Motion. In general, the only party that will file a motion is the Tenant (Although the Landlord may file a Motion for Clerk's Default and Motion for Default Judgment if the Tenant does not respond). The two main motions filed by Tenants are Motions to Dismiss and Motions to Set Rent Amount.

Whenever an eviction lawsuit is filed, the Tenant should always consider whether there are grounds to file a Motion to Dismiss. There are a number of grounds to dismiss a case, but the following are the primary ones:

1. Failure to attach the Lease or Notices. The Rules

of Procedure mandate the if the parties have a written lease, a copy of the lease must be attached to the Complaint. If it is not attached, the Complaint "fails to state a cause of action" and should be dismissed. In addition, because the Landlord is required to provide a written notice to the Tenant prior to filing the eviction action, the Notice must also be attached to the Complaint.

2. Mistakes in the Three Day Notice. There are two common mistakes you find in a three-day notice. The first is a miscalculation of dates. If the Landlord has not given the Tenant the full time required, the Notice is insufficient and grounds to dismiss the case. The second mistake is putting down the wrong amount of rent due. Under the rules, the Landlord can only ask for unpaid rent. Often the Landlord will add a late fee or utility bills. Unless there is a written lease where these items are defined as rent (or additional rent), they should not be added to the three-day notice. If the amount is incorrect the notice is improper and the case should be dismissed.

3. Mistakes in the 15-day notice. The main mistake in a 15-day notice is the failure to properly calculate the 15-day period. As mentioned earlier, the 15-day notice must be filed 15 days before the next rent payment is due. But many Landlords think it just means 15-days. So if the rent is due on the 1st of the month and the Landlord serves the 15-day notice on June 17th, he cannot file the eviction action on July 2; he must wait until August 1.

4. Improper venue. This is a rare Motion. Venue means where the case can be heard. The general rule is that an eviction case needs to be filed in the county where the property is. If the Landlord files in the wrong county, the case should be dismissed. Generally, the Court will dismiss these cases even if no Motion is filed.

5. Improper Jurisdiction. Related to venue is the concept of jurisdiction. Jurisdiction means what type of cases a Court may hear. It also indicates when a court may hear a case. The court does not have jurisdiction unless the Defendant has been served. If a defendant is never served with a lawsuit, the Court does not have jurisdiction over them and cannot hear the case. Lack of service is rare in eviction cases as service can be made personally or by simply posting on the door if nobody answers.

6. Improper party. It is important to know who you are suing. It would be surprising how many Landlords do not know who their tenants are. Often people will bring in roommates and then move out. Even more interesting is when the wrong Landlord files the eviction action. Often property will be owned by a company, but the Landlord listed in the complaint is an individual. This may occur because the owner of the company fails to separate themselves from their company. It is what is referred to as using the company as an alter ego. The owner dos not differentiate between themselves and their company and believes the two are the same. A Complaint that names the wrong party,

either Landlord or Tenant might be dismissed.

It is very important that the Landlord is careful drafting the Complaint. Normally, if the Court dismisses an eviction action the process must start over.

Aside from the Motions to Dismiss, there are other Motions that can be filed. In an eviction case based on non-payment of rent, the tenant can file a Motion to Determine Rent. As mentioned earlier, in order for the tenant to defend the eviction case, they must tender any rent due to the Registry of the Court (that just means they pay it to the Clerk of Court). However, if the tenant does not believe they should have to pay all of the rent, they can pay what they believe is proper and file a Motion with the Court explaining why they do not believe the full amount of rent should be paid, The Court will then review the Motion and make a determination as to how much rent must be paid to the Clerk. If the tenant does not pay it, the Landlord will win the case.

There are some things that are not allowed. In most civil cases the parties are allowed to do discovery. This means they are allowed to require the other pay to answer questions, to produce documents and to sit for a deposition. Because of the speed of eviction cases, discovery is not permitted as it would delay the case too long. If the landlord has also sued for back rent, the rule against discovery changes.

Any Motion (or other document) filed with the Court must also be sent to the opposing side prior to the hearing. If the opposing side is represented by an attorney, every document shall be mailed to their attorney. At the end of each Motion or other document, it is advised that the

Moving Party add a Certificate of Service.   This is a signed statement saying essentially "I certify that a copy hereof has been furnished to (here insert name or names and address or addresses of the nonmoving party of their attorney) by (delivery) (mail) (e-mail) on .....(date)......", followed by the Moving Party's signature.   The addition of this statement is deemed rebuttable proof that the pleading was provided to the Nonmoving Party.

DEFAULT AND DEFAULT JUDGMENTS

If the Tenant does not file an Answer or Motion at the end of the five day period after they have been served with the Complaint and Summons, the Landlord can seek to have the case resolved quickly through the default procedures. In order to proceed with a default judgment, the landlord must first file an Affidavit of Non-Military Service. This affidavit, a copy of which is attached in the Appendix, is a sworn affidavit that states that the Tenant is not in the military. Often Landlords will know this information directly. If not, a request can be made from the Defense Manpower Data Center (DMDC), to determine if the tenant is in the military or not. If the request is made from the DMDC, their response should be attached to the affidavit. If the Tenant is in the military, it can delay your case. The Clerk cannot issue a default until the Affidavit of Non-Military Service is filed.

Once the Affidavit has been filed, the Landlord can file a Motion for Clerk's Default (A copy is attached in the Appendix). Upon receipt of the Motion, the Clerk will review their file to ensure they have received a copy of the Return Of Service from the Sheriff showing what day the Tenant was served, calculate five days from the date of service and then check if there was anything filed before the deadline (including the incoming mail that has not yet been filed). If the review sows that no answer has been received in the required time period, the Clerk will enter a Clerk's Default (A copy is attached in the Appendix). It should be noted that while the Summons gives the Tenant 5 days to respond, they can actually file their response at any time before the Clerk's Default is issued, even if that is days or weeks after the deadline has ended.

A Clerk's Default is simply a notification that nothing has been filed. However, the ramification of this simple document are heavy. Once a Clerk's Default is filed, the Tenant cannot file any documents except a Motion to Set Aside the Clerk's Default. This Motion must show three things: 1) that the Tenant's failure to respond timely was based upon "mistake or excusable neglect" and 2) that they have a meritorious defense, and 3) that they acted promptly upon learning of the Default. If the Motion does not allege all three of these items, the Court will deny it without hearing.

Mistake or excusable neglect means that there is a valid reason for not responding. If the date was mis-calendared, or the mail was delayed, the Court may allow it. If the failure was to buy more time, or if the Tenant was trying to get an appointment with an attorney, or if the Tenant did not understand the law, those are not valid excuses.

The meritorious defense does not mean that the Tenant will win the case; it simply means that the Tenant has valid grounds to defend the case. It I not enough to allege that there are meritorious defenses- the Motion must specify what those defenses are. The Judge must have sufficient information to determine if the defenses have merit or if they are just being used to delay the case. If the clerk issues the default, but the Tenant has no defense, there is no reason to set the Default aside.

Finally, the Tenant must act promptly. You cannot "sit on your rights". Once the Tenant knows of the Default, they need to act immediately. Time is of the essence. Eviction cases are quick, so any delay could be fatal to the Tenant's defense. If the Default s set aside, the case will proceed to trial.

After the Clerk issues the Default, the Landlord then can apply for a Default Judgment. To do this, the Landlord files a Motion for Default Judgment. A draft of a Motion for Default Judgment is attached in the Appendix. This Motion needs to specify when the Tenant was served and state that the Tenant did not file a response and that the Landlord received a Clerk's Default. The Landlord should attach a copy of the Sheriff's Return of Service and a copy of the Clerk's Default. The Judge will review the Motion and if it is sufficient will grant the Default Judgment (A copy is attached in the Appendix).

DISCOVERY

Discovery is the process of gaining information from the opposing side to help build your case or expose weaknesses in the opposing party's case. While Florida has a broad and liberal discovery policy in civil court, the rules in Landlord-Tenant Law are a little different.

Generally, discovery is not allowed in eviction cases. There just isn't time to do it. Under the rules, a party generally has 30 days to respond to a discovery request. This would delay the eviction hearing too long. If, however, the Landlord also sues for back rent, discovery may be allowed for that purpose alone. This depends in part on the amount of the back rent and in part on whether the parties are represented by counsel. If the amount of back rent puts the parties in small claims court, discovery will not be allowed unless both sides are represented by counsel.

There are basically four types of discovery: Request For Production, Interrogatories, Request For Admissions and Depositions.

Request For Production: This is just what it sounds like: a request (or actually a demand) for the opposing side to provide copies of documents that are related to the case. Florida's discovery rules allow a party to request copies of documents "regarding any matter, not privileged, that is relevant to the subject matter of the pending action". That is a very broad definition. What is relevant is often up for interpretation and Plaintiffs and Defendants often disagree on this point. Even if the item requested will not be admissible in Court, if the item appears reasonably calculated to lead to admissible evidence, it is allowable. If the opposing side objects to producing documents, the requesting party must file a motion with the Court for an order compelling the production of the document.

Interrogatories: Interrogatories are written questions that the opposing party is required to answer. While the opposing party is supposed to respond to these, if they are represented by an attorney, usually the attorney will draft the answers and the opposing party will merely sign them. The answers to interrogatories may be used during the trial. Like with the Request For Production, if the opposing party objects to the Interrogatories, the requesting party can seek an Order compelling the response.

Request for Admissions: These are a series of statements that the opposing party must either admit or deny. Those items they admit do not need to be proven at the trial. If the opposing party fails to respond to a Request For Admission, the statements are deemed admitted.

Depositions: A deposition is a formal procedure where by the requesting party and opposing party meet before a court reporter. The requesting party asks the opposing party a series of questions which must be answered. If the opposing party objects to a question, they usually still must answer it. The objection is made on the record and before the deposition can be used at trial, the judge reviews the objection and rules on the admissibility of the answer. In very few circumstances can the opposing party refuse to answer a question- usually when the question involves a specific privilege such as the attorney-client privilege. However, under this circumstance, the requesting party has the right to seek an immediate hearing to get an Order compelling the other side to answer the question. If the opposing party (for example, we will say the Defendant, though this applies to both parties) fails to appear for his deposition, the Plaintiff may apply for a Writ of Bodily Attachment. This is a Court order to the local Sheriff to take the Defendant into custody to be brought before the Judge to explain why he failed to appear for the deposition. The Judge may then require the Defendant to post a bond to ensure that the Defendant complies with future discovery requests. Some judges will not issue these writs, viewing it as the same as debtor's prison which has been abolished.

If the opposing party fails or refuses to respond without sufficient grounds, along with an Order Compelling a response, they can also be sanctioned, including having to pay money to the requesting party, paying the requesting party's legal fees for both the discovery and the subsequent hearing, having pleadings or evidence stricken or in a severe case, having a judgment entered against them.

Statements made during discovery can be introduced during the trial and in some cases will be deemed to satisfy part or all of the elements of the Plaintiff's cause of action such that the Plaintiff does not need to produce any additional information.

The timelines for discovery are specifically set out in the Rules of Civil Procedure (responses to a Request To Produce, Request for Admissions and Interrogatories are due 30 days from the date of service of the discovery request or 45 days from the service of the Complaint if the discovery is requested at the same time the Complaint is filed).

Discovery is a very important part of many lawsuits and due to the complexities and importance of how it is requested and answered, it probably should not be undertaken without an attorney.

TRIAL PREPARATION

Everyone handles trial preparation differently. Some things need to be done though. If you have any witnesses that you want to testify at the trial, you should subpoena them. This is done for a few reasons. First, a subpoena will give the witness a document that reminds them when and where the trial is. Second, it gives the witness a court order they can show to their employer to get time off work. Third, and probably most important, it forces the witness to appear at the trial. If a witness tells you they will appear at trial without a subpoena and they do not appear, the Court will require you to proceed without the witness. If, however, you give the witness a subpoena, and they fail to appear at the trial, the Court can reschedule the trial and sanction the witness for failing to appear.

Witness subpoenas are issued by the Clerk of the Court. To get them, provide the name and address of the witness to the clerk. They will prepare the subpoena (there may be a slight cost). The subpoena can be served on the witness by anyone over the age of 18 who is not a party to the lawsuit.

You also need to prepare all of your evidence. Knowing what evidence you need is crucial. Without the necessary evidence, you cannot prove your case. With too much evidence, you make the case confused.

If your case is based on a written lease, you MUST have a copy. While the original is not required, it must be a signed copy, in fact, it needs to be signed by both parties. If only one side has signed it, it is not a written contract, just written evidence of a verbal contract. If you only have an unsigned copy, it is not admissible because you cannot prove that the opposing party had agreed to those specific terms.

If the defense is based on payment of rent, copies of cancelled checks should be provided. Do not rely on witnesses, unless the witness watched you hand a check to the Landlord. A witness cannot testify to something they heard, only what they saw. A witness testifying as to what they heard is generally deemed hearsay (Hearsay is any statement, including a written one, made outside of court that is offered to prove the contents of the statement).

Similarly, police reports are not admissible. All police reports are hearsay. A police report is based upon statements made to the police officer. Unless the officer actually sees an incident, he is merely reporting what other people have told him (I will discuss hearsay in more detail later when I discuss objections).

Photographs are allowed, so long as they have not been modified or altered. The photographs must reflect truthfully the appearance of what the picture is of. Generally, the person who took the picture should be present to testify that they took it and that it reflects the scene at the time they took it.

Letters and affidavits, even if notarized, are not admissible. Many people make the mistake of bringing a sworn letter or affidavit. Notarization does not make a letter valid; it just certifies the existence of the person who signed it. Notarization is necessary for a document to be recorded with the clerk of court, but it has no validity in trial. If the person is not there, they cannot be cross-examined and therefore that evidence cannot be allowed.

It also is a good strategy to write out all of the questions you need to ask your witnesses and what you are going to say as testimony. This will help prevent forgetfulness that can occur under the stress of the trial. A good way to do this is to start by listing what you MUST prove (Was there a contract? Was it signed? What are the terms? What was or was not performed? Etc.). Every cause of action in Florida has specific elements that must be proven in order for the Plaintiff to prevail. You need to know what these elements are. Then make sure your questions establish every point you need to make to establish those elements. Details are important. This is not a situation where you should try to "wing it". If you do not prove all of the necessary elements, you will not win.

How do you find the elements? There was a section on Research earlier, but for now, the easiest way is to complete a simple internet search with the type of claim you have (breach of contract, money owed, etc.) and the word "elements". A number of web sites will come up that give a list of what must be proven.

TRIAL

Many people have watched the televised court shows such as The People's Court and assume this is what going to Court is like. While the shows can be educational, they are not reflective of a true lawsuit. Televised Court show are actually arbitration hearings. They do not follow the Rules of Court. The problem with most televised court rooms is that the Judge participates too much. In Florida, by law, the Judge is allowed to assist the parties only on (1) courtroom decorum; (2) order of presentation of material evidence; and (3) handling private information. The Court is specifically instructed not to assist the parties with the accepted rules of law or to act as an advocate for either party. The Judge must stay neutral and allow the parties to present the evidence as they see fit. On the television courtrooms, the Judge acts as if they were a lawyer in many cases. They lead the parties and prompt them on how to present their case (This is not an indictment of television courtrooms. Some of the shows do explain certain evidentiary procedures and rules of court, and also can be informative as to how to present a case).

The procedure for an eviction trial is the same as for any other trial, however, it is less formal, which means some steps may be combined or even eliminated.

The first thing to notice is whether all parties are present. If the Landlord fails to appear, the case will be dismissed, and if the Tenant fails to appear, the Court will enter a default judgment against them.

Under normal practice, each party should be given a chance to make an opening statement, with the Landlord going first. This is not evidence, but merely a statement to advise the court what the party believes the evidence is going to show. In eviction cases, the Court often does away with the opening statements and goes right to the testimony. If allowed to make an opening statement, the parties should be careful not to overpromise what they will present. It is not wise to tell the Court that you will prove something during trial that you can't prove, or to make a statement when the evidence shows the opposite. The opening statements should be factual and not argumentative. They also should be fairly short.

After the opening statement, the Landlord must present their case. The Landlord always goes first, because they are the party with the burden of proof. How the case is presented is up to the Landlord. They can call witnesses and present evidence (While the rules of evidence still apply, they are enforced liberally which means the Court may not be as stringent about the manner the evidence is introduced). If the Landlord calls a witness (the Landlord is also deemed a witness if they testify) it is called direct testimony. Then, the Tenant is given the chance to question the witness, known as cross-examination. Cross examination is limited to the questions the Landlord asked. In other words, the Tenant is not supposed to bring up new issues during the cross examination (although some judges will allow it to speed up the process). If the Tenant wants to bring up new issues, they can call the same witness when it is their turn to present their case. After the Landlord is finished, they announce that they rest their case. Then, the Tenant gets to present their evidence and witnesses, allowing the Landlord to cross examine. All that being said, check with the Court as to the procedure the Court will adopt. In order to save time, the Court may have the parties present their cases at the same time so witnesses do not get called more than once.

During the testimony phase, parties can object to questions they believe are improper. Despite what you see on scripted television shows and movies, you don't just yell "Objection". An objection must have a reason and the reason must be stated. However, you need to be quick with the objection. If the question is answered, it is too late to object. Objections are made to keep information out, but also to preserve issues for appeal and to throw off the other party's rhythm. There are specific grounds to objections; you can't just say "I object because I don't like the question". Objections must be timely and specific. There are three types of objections: objections that go to questions, objections that go to the answers, and objections that go to the introduction of evidence. If an objection is made, the witness must not answer the question until the judge rules on the objection. If the judge agrees with the objection, it is "Sustained" and the witness must not answer; if the judge disagrees with the objection, it is "Overruled" and the witness must answer (witnesses cannot object).

Objections to questions mean that there is an issue with either the question that is being asked or the witness's ability to answer the question. Some of the primary Objections to questions include:

1. The question is ambiguous, confusing, misleading, vague, or unintelligible: this means that the question is not precise enough for the witness to properly answer. If ranted, the opposing party can restate the question in a way that is clearer.

2. The Plaintiff/Defendant is being argumentative: the parties question is making an argument rather than asking a question.

3. Asked and answered: This occurs when the opposing party has asked a question, it has been answered and then he asks it again, possibly in a different way (attorneys often do this in order to stress a point)

4. The question assumes facts not in evidence: Here the opposing party is adding facts to the question that have not been established yet. For example, a question could be raised about a contract, before there has been any proof that a contract existed.

5. The Plaintiff/Defendant is badgering the witness. This occurs when the opposing party is trying to provoke the witness into responding, either by mocking them or by asking questions so fast that the witness cannot answer them. This usually occurs on cross examination.

6. Best evidence rule: This objection goes to testimony about documents. If a witness is asked what terms are in a contract, the best evidence of that would be the contract itself. If the objection is allowed, the opposing party must either introduce the document in question or cease their line of questioning. This objection also goes to the originality of a document. If the opposing party attempts

to introduce a copy of a document, the best evidence rule states that the original should be introduced, not a copy.

7. Beyond the scope: This is an objection used during cross examination when the opposing party tries to discuss issues that were not raised in direct examination.

8. The question calls for a conclusion: Here the party is asking the witness not to testify about the facts, but about their opinion of the facts. While expert witnesses are allowed to testify about opinions, fact witnesses must testify to what they have seen or heard.

9. The question calls for speculation: Here the question asks the witness to guess at the answer rather than to rely on known facts.

10. The Plaintiff/Defendant has asked a compound question. This occurs when there is more than one question being asked at the same time. For example: Where did you go and what did you do?

11. Hearsay: Okay. I have mentioned hearsay several times throughout the book and now is the time to explain it. Hearsay is defined as any statement made outside of the court that is being introduced to prove the matter asserted. What does that mean? Well, law schools take weeks (or months) to teach this concept. Basically, any time a witness is testifying as to what someone else said or wrote, it is hearsay. As mentioned before, this includes police reports, because the report is merely saying what someone told the police officer, repair estimates, because the party is asking the Court to consider what a mechanic wrote. The same is true for letters and affidavits. Hearsay is not allowed because our judicial system requires that the Court allow the opposing side to cross examine witnesses. A

statement or writing made outside of the courtroom cannot be cross-examined. If the court merely accepted a police report, the opposing side would not be able to cross examine the person who described the thief to the police officer to see if she really could see the thief. If the court accepts the estimate, the opposing party could not ask the mechanic about his experience and where he derived the numbers from. It is an issue of fairness and an issue of reliability. Now, all that being said, there are twenty-four exceptions to the hearsay rule. Without going into all of them, some of the most common are: If the statement is not being admitted to prove the issue in the statement, it may be allowed. For example, if a witness testified that the sky was green, the court may allow the testimony not to prove the sky was green, but to prove the mental state of the person who said it. Or if the opposing side wants to introduce a business document, if they can show that it is a standard document that the business regularly makes and it was made during the ordinary course of business and not for the purposes of litigation, the Court may allow it. If the statement is an excited utterance or made spontaneously at the time of an event, it may be allowed as there is more reliability when things are stated immediately. If the statement was made in another court proceeding, it may be allowed. It may also be allowed if it is a statement made against one's own interest. Hearsay is one of the most common and most misunderstood and complicated of all the objections. Few lawyers know it in great detail, so don't worry if you make a mistake.

12.   The Landlord/Tenant has asked a leading question: This only applies to direct testimony as leading

questions are allowed on cross examination. A leading question is one where the answer is given to the witness. "You went to the restaurant, right?" is leading. "Where did you go?" is not.

13.		Privilege: Here the witness is protected from answering based on a specific privilege. Florida recognizes the attorney/client privilege, the psychotherapist/patient privilege, the journalist privilege, the accountant/client privilege, the sexual assault counselor/victim privilege, the domestic abuse counsellor/victim privilege, and the husband/wife privilege.

14.		The question is irrelevant or immaterial: This objection raises the issue that the question is not about the issues in the trial. Sometimes parties will try to bring in outside issues just to make the opposing side look bad, even when those things have no bearing on the case.

Objections that go to the answer are made after a witness makes a statement. They basically are asking the court or the jury to disregard what the witness has stated. The standard objections that go to the answer are:

1. Non-responsive: Here the witness has answered a question, just not the one that was asked of them.
2. Narrative: Here the witness is merely telling a story without being asked any questions. Our Court system is based on witnesses being asked questions and giving answers. While the Court may allow narrative testimony, it is not appropriate.
3. There is no question pending. Here the witness starts talking without any questions being asked of them,

Objections that go to the introduction of evidence include:

1. Lack of foundation: Here the Landlord/Tenant hasn't given enough details to warrant admitting the item into evidence. As an example, to introduce a photograph, the photographer should testify that he took the picture and that the photograph appears the same as the scene he took the picture of. This allows the court to assume that the photograph has not been tampered with. If the witness cannot state the above, the photograph should not be introduced. The same with a signed document. The party should first prove the signature on the document before introducing it into evidence.

2. Incomplete. If a party wants to introduce one page of a five-page contract, the evidence is incomplete. This objection instructs them to introduce the entire document into evidence so the court can read all of it.

3. Hearsay (addressed above)

   I have attached the standard objections at the end of this book in the Appendix.

After both sides have finished their case, they get to present their closing argument. The closing statement is a summary of what the evidence showed and an argument as to why the evidence supports that party's position. Once the closing arguments are concluded, the Court evaluates the evidence and makes a ruling. Most of the time, the Court rules from the bench; this means that the Court makes a ruling immediately. If there is any complexity to the case, the Court may take the issue "under advisement".

This means that the Court wants to take more time to evaluate the issue or research points of law before issuing a ruling. The Court then mails the final judgment to the parties.

If the Court enters judgment for the Plaintiff, they will order the Clerk of Court to issue a Writ of Possession. We will get into that process in the next section. The Court will generally also Order the Tenant to pay the Landlord's court costs, including the filing fee and the cost of service of process.

If the prevailing party hired an attorney, they can ask for an award of attorney fees, but the request must be made within 30 days of the Court's judgment, regardless of whether it is a judgment for the Landlord or the Tenant. The Court will often reserve jurisdiction on the issue of attorney fees and rule on it at a later hearing. Although you may be able to ask for fees, whether they will be granted is another question. Generally, in Florida, attorney fees are only awarded in contract cases where the contract specifically allows for attorney fees and in other cases where authorized by statute (such as security deposit cases). There are very few situations where the statutes authorize attorney fees. Before hiring an attorney, it is important to evaluate the value of the case, whether it is the type of case where attorney fees can be awarded, what the likely outcome will be and what the likely attorney fees would be. Many attorneys will give a free initial consultation and can assist with this evaluation. It is not uncommon for attorney fees to be as much or more than the judgment amount in small claims cases. It is also important to remember that in litigation, if attorney fees would be awardable to one side, they are also awardable to the other. This means that if you lose, you may have to pay the legal fees for the opposing party.

REHEARINGS, RELIEF, AND APPEALS

After the Court makes its ruling, the parties have 10 days to file a "Motion for a New Trial". This will generally not impact the eviction portion of the case, as the Tenant will have already been evicted before the Court holds a new hearing. However, it may apply if the Landlord also sued for back rent.

Under the Rules of Civil Procedure, a party may ask for a rehearing if they believe the Court ruled improperly. Improperly does not mean that the Court ruled against a party; it means that the Court contrary to the law and the evidence. A New Trial is not a right. The party requesting the new trial must provide the court with specific grounds for the new trial. The grounds necessary for a new trial are specified in the Rules of Civil Procedure and the caselaw. The grounds would include the Court misapplying the law, newly discovered evidence or the facts being misunderstood.

The ten-day time period is a strict time limit. After ten calendar days from the day the court makes its ruling, it loses the ability to order a new trial. The Court does not have to hold a hearing on the Motion for New Trial. The

Court can simply review the Motion and if the Motion does not state sufficient grounds, the Court may deny it summarily. In the alternative, the Court may decide it wants to hold a hearing and let the parties argue why the New Trial should be granted.

In certain circumstances, the ten-day rule does not apply. If there was a mistake, inadvertence or excusable neglect, or if there is newly discovered evidence that could not have been known in time to ask for a new trial, or if there was fraud, misrepresentation or misconduct by the opposing party, or if the judgment is void, or if the judgment has already been satisfied, released or vacated, then the party may ask the Court to relieve them from the final Judgment. The party must ask for relief within a reasonable time but not more than a year after the judgment was entered (unless the judgment is void or has been satisfied).

If a party believes the Court has ruled improperly, they can also request an appeal. Appeals of judgments of the Landlord-Tenant Law are heard by the Circuit Court. To seek an appeal, the party must file a Notice of Appeal within 30 days of the Judgment being rendered. Like the ten-day limit for rehearing's, the 30-day limit for an appeal is jurisdictional, meaning the Circuit Court cannot hear the appeal if the Notice is filed even a day late. Appeals are complex proceedings. I don't have the room to explain appellate procedures in detail. The shorthand explanation is as follows:

Within 30 days of the rendition of the judgment, the party who wants to appeal (called the Appellant) files a Notice of Appeal (plus applicable fees) with the Clerk of

Court.   The Notice must be in the specific format as recited in the Rules.   Within 50 days of the date the Notice is filed with the Clerk, the Clerk must prepare a copy of the file, along with an index and provide a copy of the index to each party.   Within 70 days of the filing of the Notice, the Appellant must file their "Initial Brief".   The format of the Initial brief is set out in the Rules of Appellate procedure (Either Times New Roman 14 pt font or Courier 12 pt font; double spaced with margins at least one inch; footnotes and quotes in single space, bound in book form, etc.).   The Initial Brief must contain a table of contents, a table of citations, a statement of the facts, a summary of the argument (2-5 pages in length), argument on each issue under appeal, a conclusion (no more than one page). Within 20 days of filing the Initial Brief, the opposing party (called the Appellee) must file an Answer Brief, prepared in the same manner as the Initial Brief.   Within 20 days of filing the Answer Brief, the Appellant may file a Reply Brief addressing the points raised by the Appellee in the Answer Brief. The Initial Brief and the Answer Brief may not be any longer than 50 pages.   If a Reply Brief is filed, it will be no longer than 15 pages.   Because of the highly technical format of the appellate documents, it is not recommended that the party file the appeal without the benefit of legal counsel. The Circuit Court may review the Initial Brief and determine if it has alleged grounds for reversal of the lower Court's ruling.   If not, the Circuit Court may summarily affirm the lower Court ruling and the judgment stands.   If the Circuit Court finds the Initial Brief states a cause for reversal, the Court may then review the Answer Brief to see if it shows a meritorious basis not to reverse the lower

Court's ruling. If no meritorious basis is shown, the Circuit Court may summarily reverse the lower Court ruling, sending the Judgment back to the lower Court to be corrected. If either party would like to present oral argument to the Circuit Court, it must be specifically requested when that party's last Brief is due (For the Appellant- with the Reply Brief; for the Appellee, with the Answer Brief). Each side is limited to 20 minutes of oral argument. After oral argument, the Circuit Court will generally take the issue under advisement and later issue a written ruling which is mailed to the parties.

POST JUDGMENT

So you went to Court and won your trial. Now what happens? Let's start by focusing on the eviction portion. Once the Judge signs the Judgment, it goes to the Clerk of Court for recording. The Judgment will instruct the Clerk to issue a Writ of Possession. I have attached a blank Writ in the Appendix of this book. The Writ of Possession is an Order to the Sheriff to remove the Tenant from the property. After the Clerk issues the Writ, the Landlord must take it to the Sheriff and pay the service fee. The Sheriff also needs to be given a phone number where they can reach the Landlord after the writ is served. Some Counties will also require a map showing the location of the property just as with the Summons.

The Sheriff's deputy will deliver the Writ, usually the following day. Once it has been delivered, the Deputy will call the Landlord to let them know what time the Writ was delivered. This is an important detail. The Writ gives the Tenant 24 hours to vacate the property. The Deputy will return exactly 24 hours after the Writ was posted. So if the Deputy tells the Landlord that the writ was posted on Monday at 10:00 am, the landlord needs to be at the property Tuesday at 10:00 am to meet with the Deputy. The Deputy will then knock on the door to determine if the Tenant is still inside. If there is no answer, the Deputy will go inside the unit to make sure nobody is inside. If they are, the Deputy will Order them to leave. If they refuse, they can be arrested for trespass. The Deputy will then turn over the property to the Landlord. The Landlord should immediately have a locksmith on hand to change the locks. Any property remaining in the apartment is considered abandoned and the Landlord may dispose of it (The Landlord is allowed to use security deposit funds to cover the cost of disposing the property).

If the Tenant has paid rent money into the registry of the Court, the Judge can Order it to be paid to the Landlord. After the Order is processed, the Clerk will send a check to the Landlord for the amount held (minus the Clerk's fee). What if the Judge awards the Landlord more money than the Clerk is holding? The Court helped you get the judgment, but they are not very effective in getting you paid. We do not have a debtor's prison, so the Court cannot put the opposing party in jail if they do not pay you. However, the Court can still help you collect the judgment.

First, make sure the Final Judgment includes both the Landlord's address and the Tenant's address. This is a requirement for enforcing the judgment. Then, if the rent amount is less than $5,000, ask the Court to include in the final judgment a paragraph that states: "It is further ordered and adjudged that the defendant(s) shall complete Florida Small Claims Rules Form 7.343 (Fact Information Sheet) and return it to the plaintiff's attorney, or to the plaintiff if the plaintiff is not represented by an attorney, within 45 days from the date of this judgment, unless the final judgment is satisfied or a motion for new trial or notice of appeal is filed. The defendant should not file the completed form 7.343 with the court. Jurisdiction of this case is retained to enter further orders that are proper to compel the defendant(s) to complete form 7.343 and return it to the plaintiff's attorney, or the plaintiff if the plaintiff is not represented by an attorney." The court can also require the Defendant, if he was unrepresented during trial, to attend a hearing at least 30 days after the rendition of the judgment for the purpose of testifying under oath as to their earnings, financial status and available assets.

What this does is requires the Defendant to turn over to the Plaintiff their financial status. They must disclose all of their assets and bank accounts. They must provide their employment status and other forms of income. They must supply their spouse's financial information. They have to disclose real estate, wherever located, vehicles, and loans they have made to others. If they refuse to comply, the court can hold them in contempt and increase the amount they must pay. In some places refusal to complete the form has been held a direct contempt that can subject the Defendant to jail time.

Once you have the Defendant's financial information, you can start trying to collect the judgment. You must know where their assets are before you can seize them. When the Court enters a judgment, the clerk will record it. This is going to sound redundant, but the first thing a party should do when they receive a judgment is to get a certified copy of the recorded judgment from the clerk and re-record it. This turns your judgment into an automatic lien against any real property the opposing party owns in that County. This means the judgment has to be paid off with interest if the person sells or refinances the property. There is an exception to this. Under the Florida Constitution, people's homesteads are exempt from judgments. While a judgment will create a lien on commercial or investment property, it does not create a lien on the debtor's homestead (Although, if they have a homestead, the Landlord would not be evicting them from residential property).

Next, if the Tenant is employed, the Landlord can seek a writ of continuing garnishment against the Tenant's wages. Now, this does not work if the Tenant works as an independent contractor- then there are other more timely and difficult methods to collect. But if they are an employee, the Court can order their employer to withhold up to 25% of every paycheck the employee receives until the judgment is satisfied. There is also an exception to this: If the Tenant has minor children and is the head-of-household, they are exempt from garnishment.

If the Tenant has a vehicle, such as a car, you can seize the vehicle to pay the judgment, unless the car is worth less than $1,000, is leased, or if the Tenant has not yet paid the car off. Any purchase money owed on the car will be a lien that takes priority over a money judgment. In other words, if you seize his car, you may have to pay off his loan.

If the Tenant owns other property (stereo, computers, etc.) the sheriff can seize the items and sell them at auction. The Tenant is allowed to select up to $1,000 of personal property that is exempt from sale (along with a vehicle worth less than $1,000). None of these exemptions apply to corporations; only individuals. The sheriff is authorized to seize as much as is necessary to satisfy the judgment at auction, but no more. To get the Sheriff to seize items, you will need to obtain a Writ of Execution from the Court and pay the sheriff's fee which can be several hundred dollars.

This fee is added to your judgment amount and comes off the top at the auction. You also must give the Sheriff a form called Instructions For Levy. This form describes the property the Sheriff is to seize and where it is located.

Before the Sheriff sells the items at auction, you need to make sure there are no liens on it. To do this, first go to www.floridaucc.com. This website keeps a list of secured debts. Type in the Tenant's name and if any security agreements have been recorded with them, they will come up. Review the forms (called a UCC-1) and ensure the assets the Sheriff has seized are not included on them. If so, you will need to contact the secured party as their lien is senior to the judgment lien. Next you will need to check www.sunbiz.org to ensure there are no prior judgment liens registered against the Tenant. Because judgment liens take priority based on recording dates, if there are any judgment liens recorded, you must also notify those parties. Once the Sheriff's sale occurs, the Sheriff will take his fee out of the sale proceeds. Next, he will pay the Landlord $500 for the costs, regardless of what the actual costs were. Next, the Sheriff will pay any prior judgment liens ahead of the Landlords. Finally, if there is any money left over, the Sheriff will pay that to the Landlord. If he has funds left over after the judgment has been paid, it is returned to the Tenant.

There are certain things the Landlord can seize that tend to get faster responses than others. Pets are deemed property, so seize the family pet and see how long it takes to get paid. Wedding rings are also strong incentives. If the judgment is against a business, the Landlord can seize telephone deposits and have the phones shut off until the judgment is paid.

The Landlord can also get a court order freezing the Tenant's bank account. This locks any money he has so he cannot access it until the Court can order the bank to turn the funds over to the Landlord. To do this the Landlord needs the bank location and account number.

While it sounds easy, it is not. Collecting a judgment is far more difficult than getting one. Many people are what we refer to as judgment proof. Either they have no assets, or the ones they do have cannot be seized. For example, retirement income cannot be taken. Therefore, if the judgment is against a retiree, collection may not be possible. In addition, if the Tenant has other judgments against them, the Landlord's judgment may be too far down the line to be collectable. Finally, if the Tenant files bankruptcy, all collection efforts are over (If you try to collect a debt after the debtor has filed for bankruptcy, you can be held in contempt of court by the bankruptcy court).

There are other tools that can be used to collect a judgment and luckily, Florida Statute 57.115 allows a Plaintiff to get an award of attorney fees for having to take action to collect on a judgment. This isn't absolute; the court has discretion to grant it or not. However, because of the attorney fee statute, once the Landlord has a judgment, it likely makes sense to hire an attorney to collect it.

SHOULD YOU HIRE AN ATTORNEY?

Do you need an attorney for an eviction case? No. Should you have one? It depends. Even if seeking back rent, hiring an attorney may not be cost effective. The legal fees are likely going to take a large portion of an award the Landlord gets. On the other hand, an attorney can save you time and worry. The attorney will handle all of the research, drafting and trial preparation for you.

There are several items to take into consideration when deciding if you should retain an attorney for an eviction action. First are the legal fees. Legal fees can be billed in many ways:

Hourly: The primary billing method is hourly. In an hourly billing system, the attorney keeps track of how many minutes he works on a case and bills the client based on how much time he spent. As an example, if the lawyer bills at $300 per hour and spends thirty minutes on a hearing, he will bill $150. The problem with this fee arrangement is that the legal fees will fairly quickly add up. An eviction case will easily take over three hours including meeting with clients, drafting documents, attending the trial and attending the property when the Writ is finalized. This means your fees could run to a thousand dollars or more.

Flat Fee: In a flat fee system, the attorney charges a fixed amount regardless of how much work he has to do. With the flat fee, the attorney makes the same whether he can end the case in one day or if it takes six months. The downside to this fee system is that it gives the attorney incentive to finish working more quickly, even if that is not to the client's best interest.

Contingent Fee: In a contingent fee case, the attorney gets a portion of whatever recovery the client receives. Usually the percentage is around 30% (Florida law set out a sliding scale for contingent fees that runs between 30 and 40%). Therefore, if the client receives a judgment of $1,000, the lawyer will receive around $300 of it, leaving the client with $700. This system is rarely used with Landlord Tenant cases.

Pro Bono: This is a free case for the client. Every attorney in Florida is required to do a certain amount of pro bono work or pay into a pool for others to provide free legal services. If the attorney determines that you qualify, they may be willing to work at no cost.

Second, can you get the other side to pay the fees? As mentioned earlier, in a Florida eviction action, fees are only awardable if there is a written lease with an attorney fee clause in it. Attorney fees are not awardable for verbal leases. It should be noted that if the court awards you legal fees, but the opposing party does not pay, you are still responsible for the legal fees.

Then consider whether you have the ability or desire to do the work necessary to handle the case alone. While many people have the ability, they do not have the desire; others have the desire, but not the ability. If you are not sure of the legal process and are not comfortable with doing the work yourself, it weighs in favor of hiring counsel.

Also consider whether you are the Landlord or Tenant. While the Landlord is in a positive situation, facing receiving the property and rent money or not, the Tenant is in a negative position, facing either eviction and paying money or not. While the worst the Landlord is facing in most cases is the status quo; the Tenant's worst case scenario is having to leave their apartment with 24 hours' notice. There is thus more incentive on the part of the Tenant to "lawyer up".

Finally, if the circumstances change, you may decide to hire an attorney during the course of the case, even immediately before trial begins. Once the Landlord files the Complaint, the Tenant may file a Counterclaim against them. At this point, both sides are facing a worst case scenario and may decide representation is needed.

CLOSING

Hopefully this book has provided you with some information on handling a landlord-tenant case in Florida. As mentioned at the outset, the information being provided in this book is not designed to be specific legal advice. It is offered for information purposes only. If anything you have read here has created questions regarding your situation, contact an attorney in your area. If you are not familiar with any, contact your state Bar Association for a list of local attorneys.

APPENDIX 1: 3-DAY NOTICE

Three (3) Day Notice to Pay Rent
OR DELIVER POSSESSION
<u>Residential</u>

Date: _____

TO: _____, tenant(s) and all others in possession of: _____(Street address), _____ (City), FL _____(ZIP), Tenants.

You are hereby notified that you are indebted to your Landlord, _____ in the sum of $_____ (_____ and ___/100 Dollars) for the rent and use of the premises located at _____(Street Address), _____(City), _____ County, FL _____ (ZIP), now occupied by you, and that your Landlord demands payment of the rent or possession of the premises within 3 days (excluding Saturday, Sunday, and legal holidays) from the date of delivery of this notice, to wit: on or before the _____ day of _____, 201___.

This notice is given to you pursuant to Florida Statute 83.56. **PLEASE GOVERN YOURSELF ACCORDINGLY.**

_____(Signature)
_____(Landlord's Name)

_____(Landlord's Address)
_____(City/State/ZIP)
_____(Landlord's Phone)

PROOF OF SERVICE

____ This Notice was served
        upon the person owing
        the rent.

____ The person owing the
        the rent was absent
        from their usual place
        of residence, and this Notice
        was left at said residence by
        posting.

BY:_____   DATE:_____
Name of person serving the Notice

APPENDIX 2: 7-DAY -NOTICE TO VACATE

<u>SEVEN (7) DAY NOTICE OF TERMINATION OF TENANCY</u>

DATE:

TO: _____,
tenant(s) and all others in possession of:
_____(Street address),
_____ (City), FL _____(ZIP), Tenants.
TO: _____,
tenant(s) and all others in possession of:
_____(Street address),
_____ (City), FL _____(ZIP), Tenants.

You are hereby notified that your tenancy and Rental Agreement for the above-stated rental property shall be terminated for the following material non-compliance(s) with your Rental Agreement:

_____
_____
_____

(Specify violations of Rental Agreement.

As the above-stated violations constitute an imminent threat to the health, safety, welfare and quiet enjoyment of other tenants, they also constitute material non-compliance with your Rental Agreement. This is intended as notice to you that you shall have seven (7) days from the date of delivery of this Notice to vacate the above-stated rental property, to wit: On or before the _____ day of _____, 201____. This Notice is given to you pursuant to Fla. Statutes Chapter 83. **PLEASE GOVERN YOURSELF(VES) ACCORDINGLY.**

_____(Signature)
_____(Landlord's Name)
_____(Landlord's Address)
_____(City/State/ZIP)
_____(Landlord's Phone)

PROOF OF SERVICE

____ This Notice was served
        upon the person owing
        the rent.

____ The person owing the
        the rent was absent
        from their usual place
        of residence, and this Notice
        was left at said residence by
        posting.

BY:_____   DATE:_____
Name of person serving the Notice

APPENDIX 3: 7-DAY NOTICE TO CURE

SEVEN (7) DAY NOTICE OF INTENT TO TERMINATE TENANCY

Date:

TO: _____,
tenant(s)   and   all   others   in   possession   of:
_____
(Street   address),   _____   (City),   FL
_____(ZIP), Tenants.

You are hereby notified that Pursuant to Chapter 83 of the F.S. Statutes, you are notified that you have breached material provisions of your rental agreement and/or material provisions of Chapter 83 of the Florida Statutes, in that you have:

1.   _____
_____
_____
_____
_____
____(Specify how the lease has been breached).

Demand is hereby made that you remedy the noncompliance within 7 days of receipt of this notice or your lease shall be deemed terminated and you shall vacate the premises upon such termination. If this same conduct or conduct of a similar nature is repeated within 12 months, your tenancy is subject to termination without further warning and without your being given an opportunity to cure the noncompliance. This notice is given to you pursuant to F.S. 83.56 of the Florida Statute. GOVERN YOURSELF ACCORDINGLY.

_____(Signature)
_____(Landlord's Name)
_____(Landlord's Address)
_____(City/State/ZIP)
_____(Landlord's Phone)

PROOF OF SERVICE

_____ This Notice was served
        upon the person owing
        the rent.

_____ The person owing the
        the rent was absent
        from their usual place
        of residence, and this Notice
        was left at said residence by
        posting.

BY:_____
     DATE:_____
Name of person serving the Notice

APPENDIX 4: 15-DAY NOTICE

FIFTEEN DAY NOTICE OF TERMINATION OF TENANCY

DATE:

TO: _____ (Tenant's name) and all others in possession of:

_____ (Street address), _____(City), _____ County, Florida, Tenant.

You are hereby notified that your month-to-month tenancy/lease of the above-stated rental property is terminated effective _____, 201____. You shall vacate the above-stated rental property on or before midnight _____, 201____. This notice is given to you pursuant to Florida Statutes Sec. 83.57. PLEASE GOVERN YOURSELF ACCORDINGLY.

_____(Signature)
_____(Landlord's Name)
_____(Landlord's Address)
_____(City/State/ZIP)
_____(Landlord's Phone)

PROOF OF SERVICE

____ This Notice was served
      upon the person owing
      the rent.

____ The person owing the
      the rent was absent
      from their usual place
      of residence, and this Notice
      was left at said residence by
      posting.

BY:_____   DATE:_____
Name of person serving the Notice

APPENDIX 6: 5-DAY SUMMONS

IN THE COUNTY COURT
IN AND FOR _____ COUNTY, FLORIDA

Plaintiff-Landlord,

vs.   CASE NO.:

Defendant-Tenant.
_____/

RESIDENTIAL EVICTION SUMMONS (5 days)

TO: _____(Tenant's Name)
    _____(Tenant's Address)
    _____(City/State/ZIP)

PLEASE READ CAREFULLY

You are being sued by_____
(Landlord's name) to require you to move out of the place
where you are living for the reasons given in the attached
complaint.

You are entitled to a trial on the eviction count to decide whether you can be required to move, but you MUST do ALL of the things listed below. You must do them within FIVE (5) days (not including Saturday, Sunday, or any legal holiday) after the date these papers were given to you or to a person who lives with you or were posted at your home.

THE THINGS YOU MUST DO ARE AS FOLLOWS:

1.   Write down the reasons why you think you should not be forced to move. The written reasons must be given to the court clerk at the _____ County Courthouse;

2.   Mail or take a copy of your written reasons to:

_____(Landlord's Name)
_____(Landlord's Address)
_____(City/State/ZIP)

3.   Give the court clerk the rent that is due. You MUST pay the clerk the rent each time it becomes due until the lawsuit is over. Whether you win or lose the lawsuit, the judge may pay this rent to the landlord. Failure of the Tenant to pay the rent into the registry of the Court as provided herein constitutes an absolute waiver of the Tenant's defenses other than payment and the Landlord is entitled to an immediate default without further notice of hearing thereon.   Any payment into the registry of the Court must be tendered in cash, cashier's check or money order and must be accompanied by payment of the clerk's registry fee of two (2) percent of the first five hundred dollars ($500.00) deposited and one (1) percent of any amount above five hundred dollars ($500.00).

4.   If you and the landlord do not agree on the amount of rent owed, give the court clerk the money you say you owe. Then before the trial you must ask the judge to set up a hearing to decide what amount should be given to the court clerk.

IF YOU DO NOT DO ALL OF THESE THINGS WITHIN 5 WORKING DAYS YOU MAY BE EVICTED WITHOUT A HEARING OR FURTHER NOTICE

In accordance with the Americans with Disabilities Act, persons with disabilities needing a special accommodation to participate in this proceeding should contact Court Administration not later than seven days prior to the proceeding at the _____ County Courthouse,

_____
_____(Courthouse address and telephone).

THE STATE OF FLORIDA:
To Each Sheriff of the State:

YOU ARE COMMANDED to serve this summons and a copy of the complaint in this lawsuit on the above-named defendant.

DATED on this _____ day of _____, 201___.

_____
As Clerk of the Court

APPENDIX 7: 20-DAY SUMMONS

IN THE COUNTY COURT
IN AND FOR _____ COUNTY, FLORIDA

Plaintiff-Landlord,

vs.   CASE NO.:

Defendant-Tenant.

_____/

SUMMONS: PERSONAL SERVICE ON AN
INDIVIDUAL

TO: _____(Tenant's Name)
     _____(Tenant's Address)
     _____(City/State/ZIP)

IMPORTANT

A lawsuit has been filed against you. You have 20 calendar days after this summons is served on you to file a written response to the attached complaint/petition with the clerk of this circuit court, located at: Clerk of Court,

_____

_____(Courthouse address).

A phone call will not protect you. Your written response, including the case number given above and the names of the parties, must be filed if you want the Court to hear your side of the case.

If you do not file your written response on time, you may lose the case, and your wages, money, and property may be taken thereafter without further warning from the Court.
There are other legal requirements. You may want to call an attorney right away. If you do not know an attorney, you may call an attorney referral service or a legal aid office (listed in the phone book).

If you choose to file a written response yourself, at the same time you file your written response to the Court, you must also serve a copy of your written response on the party serving this summons at:

_____(Landlord's Name)
_____(Landlord's Address)
_____(City/State/ZIP)
_____(email address)

If the party serving summons has designated e-mail address(es) for service or is represented by an attorney, you may designate e-mail address(es) for service by or on you. Service must be in accordance with Florida Rule of Judicial Administration 2.516. Copies of all court documents in this case, including orders, are available at the Clerk of the Circuit Court's office. You may review these documents, upon request. You must keep the Clerk of the Circuit Court's office notified of your current address.

THE STATE OF FLORIDA:
To Each Sheriff of the State:

YOU ARE COMMANDED to serve this summons and a copy of the complaint in this lawsuit on the above-named defendant.

Albert L. Kelley, Esq.

DATED on this _____ day of _____, 201___.

_____
As Clerk of the Court

APPENDIX 8: NON-MILITARY AFFIDAVIT

IN THE COUNTY COURT
IN AND FOR _____ COUNTY, FLORIDA

_____
      Plaintiff-Landlord,

vs.   CASE NO.:

_____
      Defendant-Tenant.
_____/

<u>NON-MILITARY AFFIDAVIT</u>

STATE OF FLORIDA
COUNTY OF MONROE

     BEFORE ME, the undersigned authority, personally appeared _____ (Landlord's Name), who being first duly sworn deposes and says that to the best of his information, knowledge and belief, the Defendant-Tenant, _____ (Tenant's name) is not currently in the military service.
     FURTHER, AFFIANT SAYETH NOT.

_____
(Landlord's Signature)

STATE OF FLORIDA   )
COUNTY OF _____)

　　　　　SWORN TO AND SUBSCRIBED before me this _____ day of _____, 201____.

　　　　　　　　　　　　　　　_____
　　　　　　　　　　　　　　　Notary Public
　　　　　　　　　　　　　　　Commission No.

　　　　　　　　　　　　　　　(SEAL)

Personally known _____　　　　　OR　　　　　Produced
Identification _____

Type of Identification Produced: _____

DID NOT take Oath _____　OR　DID take Oath _____

APPENDIX 9: MOTION FOR CLERK'S DEFAULT

IN THE COUNTY COURT
IN AND FOR _____ COUNTY, FLORIDA

_____
Plaintiff-Landlord,

vs.   CASE NO.:

_____
Defendant-Tenant.
_____/

MOTION FOR CLERK'S DEFAULT

Plaintiff-Landlord, _____,

moves for entry of a default by the Clerk against

_____, the

Defendant, for failure to serve any paper on the

undersigned or file any paper as required by law.

Respectfully submitted,

_____(Signature)
_____(Landlord's Name)
_____(Landlord's Address)
_____(City/State/ZIP)
_____(Landlord's Phone)

APPENDIX 10: CLERK'S DEFAULT

IN THE COUNTY COURT
IN AND FOR _____ COUNTY, FLORIDA

_____

     Plaintiff-Landlord,

vs.   CASE NO.:

_____

     Defendant-Tenant.

_____/

CLERK'S DEFAULT

A default for the purposes of possession is entered in this action against the Defendant named in the foregoing action for failure to serve or file any paper as required by law.

Dated this ___ day of _____,
201____.

_____

As Clerk of the Court

APPENDIX 11: MOTION FOR DEFAULT JUDGEMENT

IN THE COUNTY COURT
IN AND FOR _____ COUNTY, FLORIDA

_____

Plaintiff-Landlord,

vs.   CASE NO.:

_____

Defendant-Tenant.

_____/

MOTION FOR DEFAULT JUDGMENT

COMES NOW the Plaintiff,

_____ by and through

his undersigned counsel, and moves this Honorable

Court for entry of a Default Judgment against

Defendant, _____, and in

support thereof states:

    1.   On _____, 201___,

Plaintiff filed suit against Defendant.

    2.   Defendant was served with the Summons

and Complaint on _____ ___, 201____.

    3.   Defendant had Five days from date of

service to respond to the Complaint.   This five-day

period ran on _____ ____, 201___.

    4.   On _____ ____, 201___, Plaintiff

received a Clerk's Default.

    5.   Plaintiff is entitled to an order of eviction

and an award of court costs.

    WHEREFORE, Plaintiff prays for entry of a

default judgment for eviction, the issuance of a Writ of

Possession, costs, and for such further relief as this court

deems just and proper.

Respectfully submitted,

_____(Signature)
_____(Landlord's Name)
_____(Landlord's Address)
_____(City/State/ZIP)
_____(Landlord's Phone)

APPENDIX 12: DEFAULT JUDGEMENT

IN THE COUNTY COURT
IN AND FOR _____ COUNTY, FLORIDA

_____
    Plaintiff-Landlord,

vs.   CASE NO.:

_____
    Defendant-Tenant.
_____/

DEFAULT JUDGMENT FOR EVICTION AND POSSESSION OF RESIDENTIAL PREMISES

THIS CAUSE having come before the Court for

consideration on _____ _____, 201___

upon Plaintiff's Motion for Default Judgment, and the

Court being fully advised in the premises, it is hereby:

ORDERED AND ADJUDGED that:

1.   Judgment in favor of Plaintiff and against Defendant is hereby entered for eviction and possession of the rental premises located at

_____

_____,

for which Writ of Possession shall issue forthwith.

2.   Court costs in the amount of

_____ Dollars

($_____) are awarded in favor of the Plaintiff and against the Defendants, which shall incur interest at the highest amount allowed by law.

DONE AND ORDERED in Chambers in

_____, _____ County,

Florida, this ____ day of _____,

201___ for which let execution issue.

_____

COUNTY JUDGE

APPPENDIX 13: TRIAL OBJECTIONS

TRIAL OBJECTIONS LIST
1. The Form of Question:
    a. Leading
    b. Argumentative
    c. Confusing
    d. Unintelligible
2. Subject Matter Of Question:
    a. Assumes fact not in evidence
    b. Asked and answered
    c. Beyond scope of direct [or cross exam or redirect or recross]
    d. Insufficient foundation for hypothetical
3. Substance Of The Evidence Sought:
    a. Hearsay
    b. Irrelevant
    c. Violation of best evidence rule
    d. Question calls for conclusion
    e. Self-serving
    f. Violates Parol Evidence Rule
    g. Document speaks for itself
    h. Not qualified to give answer
    i. Invades province of jury
4. Incompetence of Witness to Answer or Exhibit to Be Received:
    a. Rule 701, 702; Rule 601 (a) and (b)
5. Failure to Lay Proper Foundation :
    a. Inadequate qualifications of witness: expert
    b. Inadequate preliminaries for substance of

conversation

    c. Mental capacity of child of tender years not established

    d. Inadequate premise established for opinion

6. **Failure to Lay a Proper Foundation for Intro of Exhibit:**

    a. Posed photograph

    b. Lack of proof that conditions are same

    c. Material variance

    d. Foundation for Exhibit lacks reliability

    e. Failure to establish mechanical reliability of machine

7. **Impropriety of Circumstance**:

    a. Answer nonresponsive

    b. Court refuses to give instructions tendered

    c. Court to giving instruction tendered by opponent over objection

    d. Objectionable comments by opposing counsel during opening statement or closing argument

    e. Asking prejudicial or improper questions

    f. Improper conduct of counsel

    g. Prejudicial conduct of Judge

    h. Improper display of Exhibit not received into evidence

i. Making improper remarks while registering objection

APPENDIX 14: WRIT OF POSSESSION

IN THE COUNTY COURT
IN AND FOR _____ COUNTY, FLORIDA

_____
    Plaintiff-Landlord,

vs.   CASE NO.:

_____
    Defendant-Tenant.

_____/

<u>WRIT OF POSSESSION</u>
THE STATE OF FLORIDA:

To All and Singular the Sheriffs of said State:

    YOU ARE HEREBY COMMANDED to remove the Defendant _____
from the following described property in
_____ County, Florida, said writ to issue forthwith:

_____

_____

and to put Plaintiff in full possession thereof.

      WITNESS my hand and the seal of said Court on this _____ day of _____, 201____.

                _____
                Clerk, County Court

ABOUT THE AUTHOR

ALBERT L. KELLEY, is an attorney, author, book publisher, film producer, traveler and adventurer located in Key West, Florida. His law practice concentrates primarily in the areas of business, corporations, contracts, copyright, trademark, and entertainment law, as well as foreclosure defense.   He graduated cum laude from Florida State University College of Law in 1989. He served for years as an adjunct professor for St. Leo University in their Business Administration program, teaching courses in business, employment and administrative law. For six years Al wrote a weekly business law newspaper column and has authored books on business law and small claims court. He has also been a featured panelist at Florida State University's College of Law's Annual Entertainment Art and Sports Law Symposium. Albert L. Kelley serves as legal counsel for the world's largest offshore powerboat race promoter as well as museums, art galleries, television stations, performers and newspapers. On the business side, Albert is corporate counsel to over 150 corporations, and has filed over 60 trademark registrations and countless copyright applications. Albert has negotiated contracts with numerous national companies including Apple Computers, Harley Davidson, and Ralston Purina. Al has given numerous seminars on trademarks, copyrights, film licensing and financing, and foreclosure defenses. He is a licensed skydiver, hang-glider pilot, and scuba diver.

CPSIA information can be obtained
at www.ICGtesting.com
Printed in the USA
LVHW021512191122
733280LV00027B/1990

9 781945 772108